About Greg Bright

'Born in Wales in 1951, I was making mazes six years later.
I did intensive work on mazes until I was ten. This period
saw the instigation of the "Hole" technique and the
development of a rudimentary "Colour-maze" system.
For some years following, there was a partial hiatus in my
mazeological pursuits, though I kept my hand in by
occasionally constructing mazes out of wood, rubber bricks,
books, plasticine and furniture. For a time, I kept some white
mice expressly for the purpose of research. It was not until I
was nineteen that I had fully recovered from a wasted
decade in that pernicious and degrading institution –
school. I had indulged in various disparate activities for a
couple of years, notably making compartmented boxes and
playing with the Scratch Orchestra, when, in 1971,
I concentrated my energies and dug the "Pilton Maze".
Now, after another three years of unbroken maze work
(including two "Colour-mazes" and two books) I see that I have
only touched on the potential of this phenomenon.'

Greg Bright, 1975

In the spring of 1978, the "Longleat Maze" (designed
by Greg Bright for Lord Weymouth) was completed and
opened to the public. This is the largest and most
sophisticated maze in the world. Currently Bright is
working on two books: a "Hole-maze" to be published by
Fontana in 1979 and "Ten TV Plays". His earlier works
include "Greg Bright's Maze Book" and "Visual Music", both
published by Latimer.

GREG BRIGHT'S FONTANA MAZES

Fontana/Collins

First published in Fontana 1975

5 6 7 8 9 10

Made and Printed in Great Britain by
William Collins Sons & Co Ltd Glasgow

Introduction

low me to introduce you to the Mazes. Reader, Mazes; Mazes, Reader. Charmed? I am glad.
, I am the first to admit that these anfractuous gems are not without their flaws, but then
rfection is as lifeless as alabaster and so I am content. But what are they, these puzzles? Are they
ys? Are they art? They are toys if you choose to play with them. As for art, I should hardly wish to
andon them to that inelegant category of meagre intoxication. I have introduced them as Mazes,
d that will do. Treat them as you please; that is my policy.

cently, a sizeable art exhibition included a novel olfactory piece. The artist responsible for this
orous exhibit apparently holds the opinion that man's aesthetic endeavours, while more than
equately indulging the eyes and ears, brazenly ignore the nose. Quite what Harry Wheatcroft or
. Rothschild would make of this particular artist's singular conclusions is a point worthy of
eculation. As for the average cosmetics magnate, one can almost hear the jaw drop. Perhaps our
tist has in mind the absence of olfactory titillation in the context of the picture gallery. Though,
reflection, it would be as pertinent to remark how rarely one sees oil paintings or small bronzes,
nked in the Pouilly Fuisse while partaking of the fish course. No, there is nothing new under the
n; notwithstanding that this apparent lack of novelty is largely due to the idiosyncracies of
assification, it being hardly less fecund to adopt the view that everything under the sun simply
ows with newness.

These animadversions are not entirely without purpose. Hopefully they will serve to qualify my imminent claim to originality. For many years, I have been developing the art of 'routing', the mc recent examples of which lie but leaves away. 'Ah! But what about the legendary Maze at Knossc where Theseus slew the Minotaur?', you demand. 'What about the great Eighteenth century Maz at Versailles! What of Spaghetti Junction? What –' 'What about children's puzzle book Mazes?', anticipate you correctly. Yes? Well, this latter puerile manifestation of the Maze form is sufficier separated from my work by its quality (or rather the lack of it), as to render any deeper search for schism redundant. The legendary maze of King Minos is just that – legendary, and pays scarcely more homage to reality than Icarus's presumptuous solar-cursed flight, while the Eighteenth century European Mazes were ornamental walks designed by gardeners better equipped to deal w roots of a different nature. Your reference to Spaghetti Junction is possibly the most germane comparison. However, the distinction of motives renders the civil engineers and I no more than distant cousins.

But perhaps you were persuaded of the novelty of my work all along, and my arguments have don nothing except plant the seeds of doubt. Such are the hazards inherent in attempting to communicate with those you cannot see and do not know. How can I speak simple words of truth once to the air and to countless unique individuals – if my public may be so described? Well, for those who need no fillip to acknowledge the originality of the art of routing, perhaps the above wi have served to heighten their conception of its significance. For though few among my readers ill be unfamiliar with the fundamental idea of a labyrinth, for most this opportunity of a direct onfrontation with such involute pearls as adorn the pages of this book will be unprecedented. he purpose, then, of this self-administered exordial panegyric is largely to augment the status of ae Maze in the eyes of the reader and thereby constrain any misconceptions that inexperience ay have fostered.

he items in this collection pay less attention to overall structural theories than my earlier work. have used a more pragmatic approach in their construction. Instead of making a schematic diagram mutually accessible centres inlaid with partial valves and subsequently convoluting the entire stem, I have worked in a raw, more organic way, generating and harnessing the junction forces ee M 33). The Mazes are arranged in ascending difficulty, with concessions made to structural ad graphic variety. For their exploration I recommend a sharpened match. Misdemeanours, such jumping back to the start and from one point to another or trying to work the route back from the ad, are, frankly, degrading. The impatient and suspicious may find satisfaction in the solutions at e back of the book, the competitive in swords of speed; (par timings are ruled out by the puzzles' on-conformist behaviour). Throughout, brief notes provide a Virgil to your Dante.

was the mystery of Mazes that originally attracted me to them; the euphoria of bewilderment, e strangenesses of their vertiginous curves and recondite routes. But the love-affair is over; I have ened their secrets. Now, I am pimping for them. Can I tempt you, dear Reader?

M1 Door Panels

While forcibly prone in '73

by

craning

my

neck

and peering over my sprawled form, I could manage to glimpse the door.

M2 Door Panels

M3

COMMENCING AT THE CLEARING LOCATED AT THE UPPER APEX, GET TO THE ISOLATED SQUARE BELOW

_____ ✳ *

_____ ✳ *

_____ ✳ *

* Three titles, submitted by that emitter of 'warp therapy',
  The Phantom Captain, omitted as a matter of form.

M4

IN AT THE BOTTOM TO THE SPACE JUST ABOVE IT

M5

M6 Sixteen Paths

This maze is called Sixteen Paths
because it is comprised of sixteen paths.
The paths weave under and over each other.

FROM THE CENTRAL
TRIANGLE

TO THE
SATELLITE

M7 Quarter Aureole

FROM THE RIGHT-HAND ED

SLIDE

DOWN,

DOWN

AND

DROP

OUT

OF

THE BOTTOM

M8 The Chameleon's Eye

PROD
THE
PUPIL

M9 Islands

TO THE SPACE JUST OFF TOP CENTRE

FROM THE CENTRAL SPACE

The central space can be seen as
a single undivided area containing four islands.
The whole maze may be looked at in this way,
the other islands are merely harder to negotiate.

M10 Quincunx

START BANG IN THE MIDDLE

AND AIM

FOR THE

CUL-DE-SAC

AT THE CENTRE OF THE BOTTOM LEFT QUARTER

M11 Naja

FROM THE CENTRE TO THE BULB ABOVE

M12 Sidereal Clock (Artist's Impression)

Apart from pointing out that the start is in the centre,
I have nothing to say about this maze, so just
to keep the ball rolling and hint at my caprice,
reproduced below are the lyrics to a little number
I wrote back in the Summer of '74.

Eupractic Woman: Panurgic Man   7 Aug. '74

When a panurgic man
Meets a eupractic woman
You know the sparks have got to fly
Expect a dazzling duet
From this coruscating couple
It's going to light up the night
   Oh, eupractic woman, I'm a panurgic man

Well, the stage is set
In the great outdoors
Right by the camp-fire glow
She fell asleep in my arms
As the stars weaved their charms
Around the twinkle of a super-nova
   Oh, eupratic woman, I'm a panurgic man

Like a welder at his torch
We dared not remove our masks
The darkened glass was vital to our sight, you see
Were we banished to a vortex?
Did spectres line my cortex?
Had we vanished in a naked singularity?
   Oh, eupractic woman, I'm a panurgic man

And when the explosion
Was just so much debris
The turbulent firmament galvanised
For the final word
On these impeccable pyrotechnics
We were confused, sublimated, polarised.

M13 Miss Riley's Plumbing

TOP
LEFT
BOX

TO BOTTOM RIGHT BOX

'*In this domestic waterway, live shoals of microscopic fish (collectively, the naked eye perceives them as pale shadows in the periphery of vision). However, these elusive creatures are extremely shy and a direct glance will cause them to conceal themselves behind the nearest overlapping pipe.*'

From: *Op Can Be Twee*, ch. 5

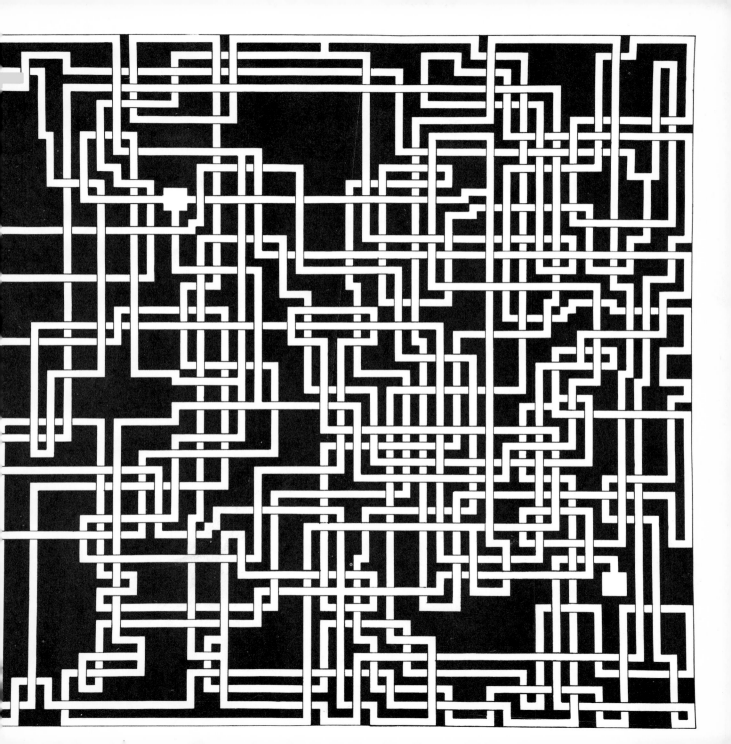

M14 Supermatricial Tectonics

'Basically, the idea is that you enter, filled with confidence and good intentions on the right hand side, and emerge with nerves like wet cotton wool three days later through the gap in the frame on the left hand side.
The round trip has been specially designed to be so aggravating that in the process, thoughts of bank overdrafts, mortgage rates and the price of Scotch pale into insignificance.'

From: *Morning Telegraph*

M15 The Hexagonal One

The following is an extract from 'The Law of The Game of Earth'
© Greg Bright 1971.

7. THE NATURE
(ii) *The Spiral of Oscillating Decisions*

The quality of decisions is independent of their identity. To illustrate this, let me use as an example the simple game of guessing in which hand a person has placed a stone. Let 'G' be guessing, and 'C' be concealing the stone. Say, for example, on the first round 'G' makes a guess and 'C' shows the stone to be in his right hand. 'C' then rearranges the stone. 'G' considers: 'If "C" is simple-minded, he will re-perform the ritual, changing nothing; therefore, retaining the stone in his right hand. If, however, he is of slightly subtler mind, he will alter the arrangement in order to confuse me; therefore, placing the stone in his left hand. Supposing his mind is of yet greater subtlety and he considers me of slightly subtle thought, he may think, "Ah, 'G' thinks that I will place it in my left hand to confuse him, so I'll place it in my right hand and he will guess wrong." Therefore, the stone will be in his right hand.' With increasing subtlety of mind, and greater estimation of his respective opponent, the decisions of 'G' and 'C' oscillate, spiralling outward, each alternate left or right decision being composed of higher thought than its predecessor. Thus, while actually a decision remains invariable, the quality of thought governing it is susceptible to infinite variation. This basic principle is manifest in 'Earth', though the spirals are multiple and inter-locking. Victory lies not in making a particular decision or in deciding from a higher vantage point than one's opponent, but in realisation of the rhythm of the play, and in placing one's decision on the appropriate loop of the spiral. It can readily be seen that the intellect does not have the power to unravel the vast interfusion of spirals; decisions must be left to the intuition.

To avoid the inevitability of choice, one must have perfect fluidity, neither 'choosing' nor 'choosing not to choose': riding the paradox, motionless with equivalent velocity, limitless in total harmony.

M16 Over the Edge

See the tiny gap? – In ther

See the clearir

where you finisl

No, it's over the edg

Behold the vaulted biosphere!

– That noble hub
twixt quark and quasar; the hand of pattern
is ever at Chaos's throat.

FROM THE OUTSIDE TO THE WHITE BULB

M18 Phased Matrices: Imperial/Metrical

BISHOP'S HAT

DUE NORTH TO THE

FROM THE
CENTRAL
COURTYARD

More and more I encounter echoes of the Matrix.
The Matrix is fast becoming ubiquitous.
From that it is only a short   step
to being omnipresent, the very grain of the void.*

*Foreign term for the lot.

M19 Medium Focus Perspective Matrix

FROM THE WHITE ARROW-HEAD (UPPER LEFT) TO THE WHITE RHOMBUS (LOWER RIGHT)

'*Weren't you lucky to find a field in which to dig the Pilton Maze!*'

'Lucky? I feel I am responsible for everything that happens to me, good or bad.'

'*What? Do you want to carry the whole world on your shoulders?*'

'Are you referring to the lump that's hanging off the bottoms of my shoes?'

M2O

UNDER AND UP

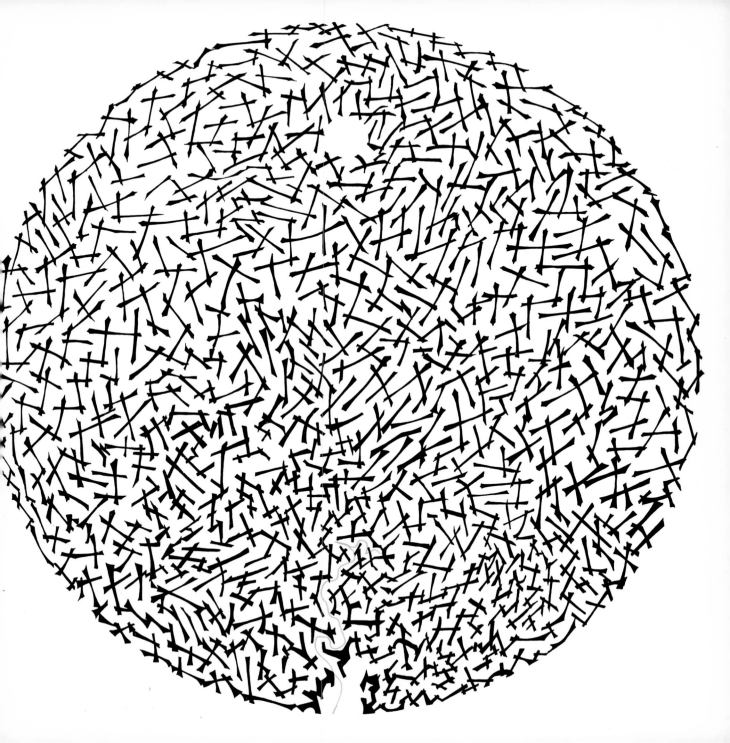

M21 Twin Hexagons

END IN THE CENTRE OF THE LEFT

BEGIN IN THE CENTRE OF THE RIGHT.

M22 Lumberjack's Nightmare

PITH TO BARK

And talking of trees, there were these two dogs, and one
said to the other, 'Have you heard the one about the two sheep?'
'No,' replied the other dog, 'Well,' said the first dog,
'There were these two sheep, and one sheep said to the other,
"There were these two cows, and one said to the other . . ." '
'That is absurd!' broke in the other dog, 'Cows can't talk!'

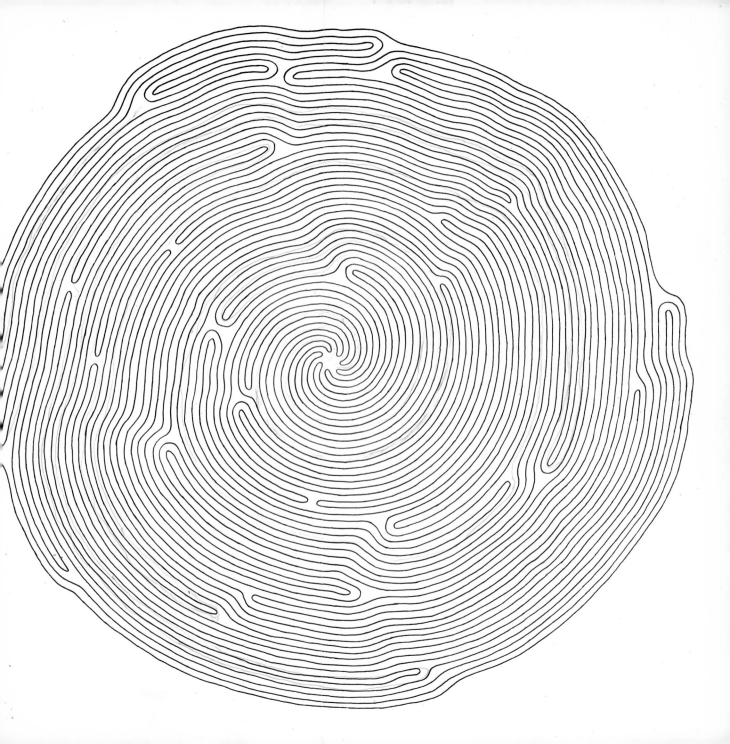

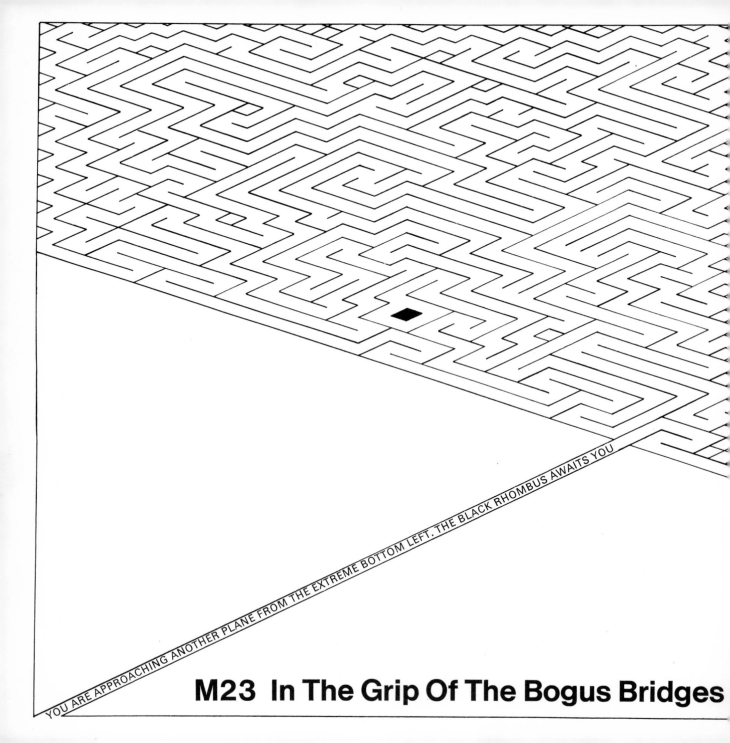

YOU ARE APPROACHING ANOTHER PLANE FROM THE EXTREME BOTTOM LEFT. THE BLACK RHOMBUS AWAITS YOU

M23 In The Grip Of The Bogus Bridges

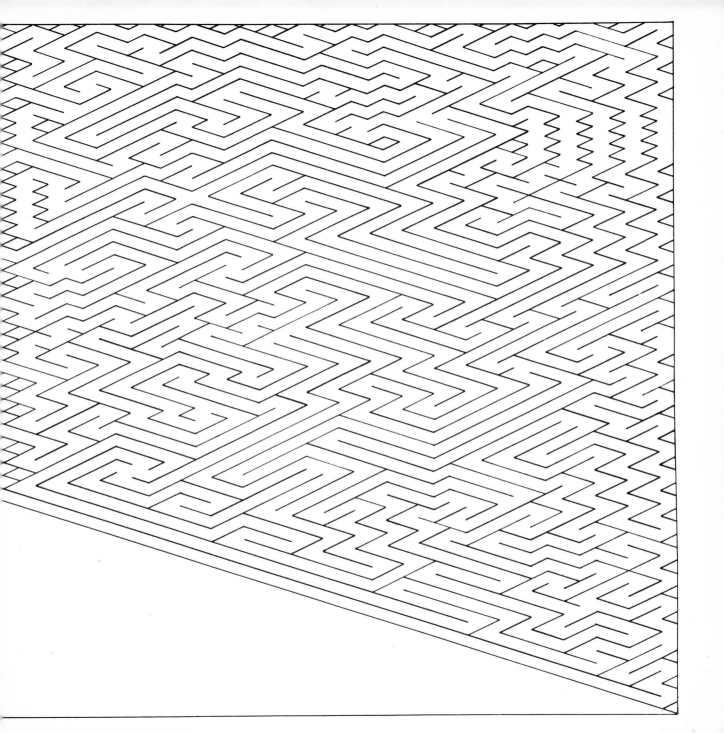

M24 The Badge of Hell

YOU
ARE
IN
THE
DARKEST
PIT

M25 Reciprocal Fibonacci

EXIT LEFT

ENTER RIG

This matrix is based on a reciprocal form of the Fibonacci
series. It was while returning to this familiar mathematical
phenomenon for the composition of the matrix, that my
thoughts were led by association to realise that waning
fashionableness can provide some of the most decadent and
piquant tokes of the lot. Like the exquisite stench of a
bad joke, my predilection for which qualifies the attempts
at humour prevalent in this book.

M26 The Coy Helix

(Note the 'inappropriateness' of having a non-logarithmic spiral
to complement the following paragraph.
See: *The Spiral of Oscillating Decisions* M 15)

CENTRE SQUARE TO BOTTOM RIGHT EQUIVALENT

Paradoxically, the Paradox (or 'Swinging
Syzygy'), while appearing to be *the* culminal
conceptual synthesis, is nothing more than an
expedient towards inducing, or a linguistic
manifestation of, an incipient transcendental
mode of classification; so inherent caducity
exposes its captious role as crux. But
remember, contradiction can be either self-
annihilatory or dynamic: thus, the *dynamic*
paradox can relinquish its ephemerality by means
of *acceleration*. However, this is a mute point.

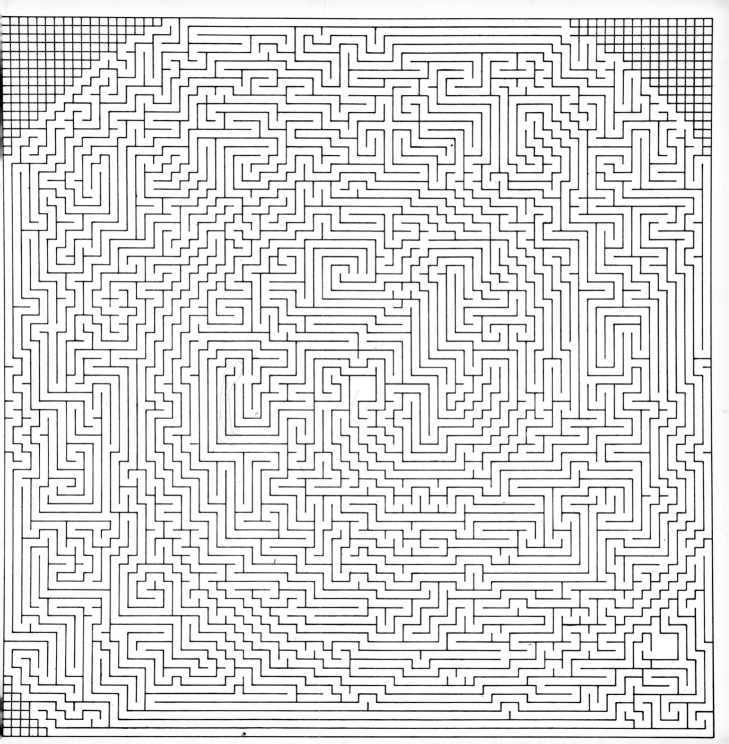

M27

FROM THE CENTRE OUT

M28 The Cube

```
FROM
THE
RHOMBOID
WINDOW IN THE LEFT HAND FACE TO ITS COUNTERPART OVER
                                                    ON
                                                    THE
                                                    RIGHT

                                                    VIA
                                                    THE
                                                    BLACK
                                                    PATHS
```

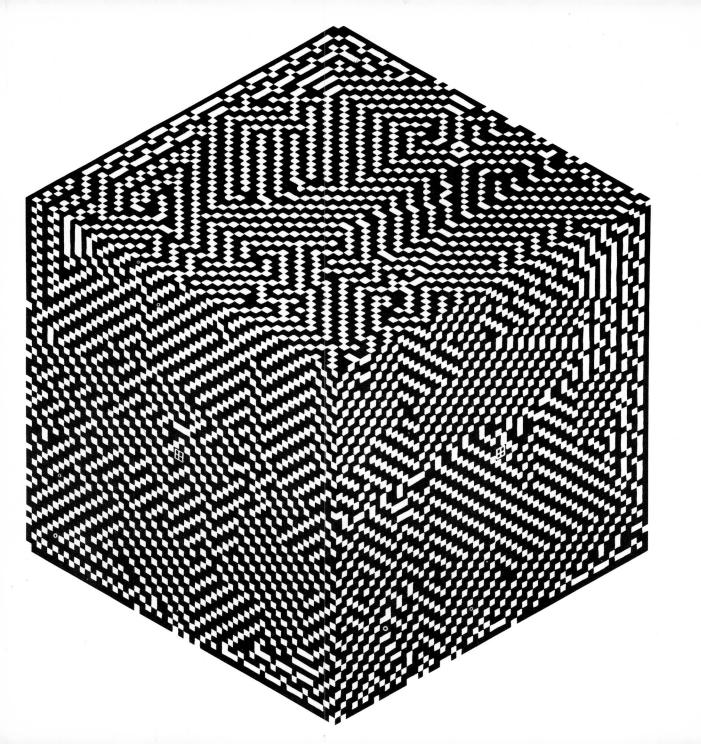

M29 Sisyphus Was Here

The logic of metaphysical speculation is inevitably tautologous; a man trying to look himself in the face – without a mirror! The amount by which a given piece of reasoning avoids being sophistical is a function of its projected awareness of the fact that it only – makes itself. (The other vector determining its quality being that of the fineness of its composition.) Philosophers part the curtain with varied and splendid gestures, but they reveal – nothing. Ideas lack immediacy. If it is not obvious, it is not worth saying; the obvious is the only important thing that we may miss.

STARTING ANYWHERE TRAVEL ANTICLOCKWISE AND RETURN TO FROM WHENCE YOU CAME

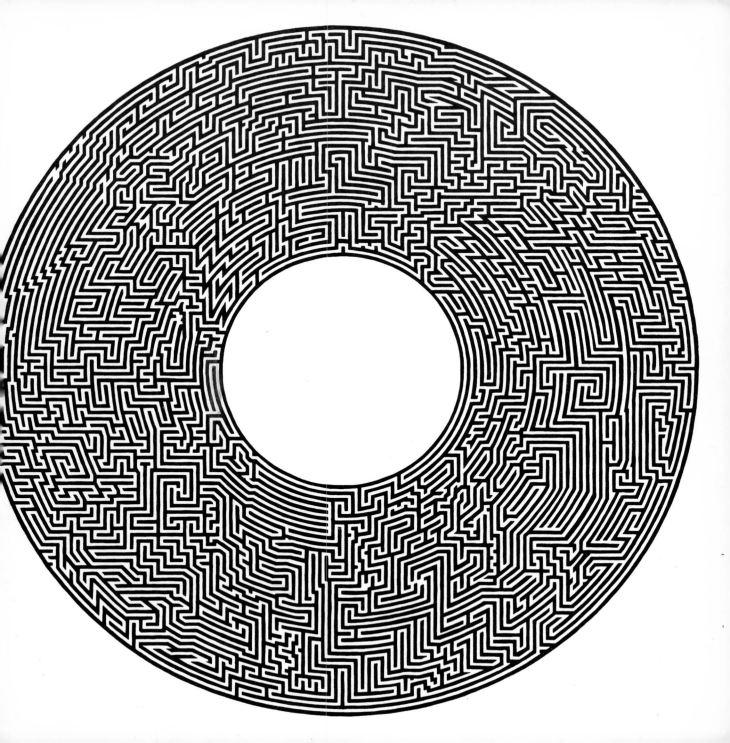

M30 Fresh Muzz

I hope this is a suitably Op-artistish* title.

THERE IS A GAP IN THE BOTTOM THAT LEADS TO THE CENTRE

*Try saying that after a few gin and tonics.

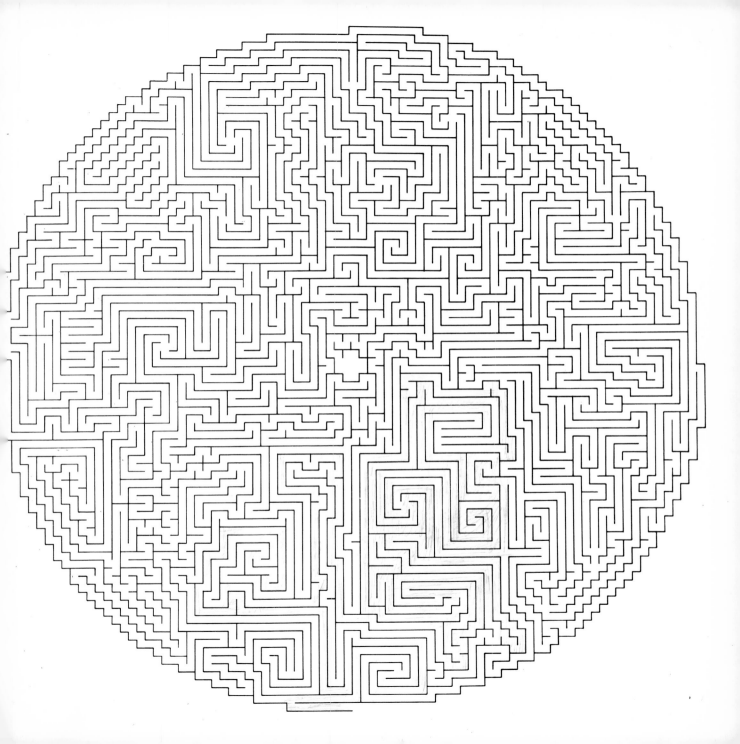

M31

TO THE BLACK HEXAGON OVERHEAD

FROM THE DOTTED RHOMBUS
(the 'reclining diamond' for the poetic,
the 'middle' for the prosaic)

The paths weave under and over each other.

M32 The Plush Octagon

STARTING AT THE BLACK RHOMBUS   EVENTUALLY PASS OUT   VIA THE GAP, CENTRE RIGH

(the poetic and prosaic can do-it-yourself)   (and here a notice to the hasty interpreter not to lose consciousne

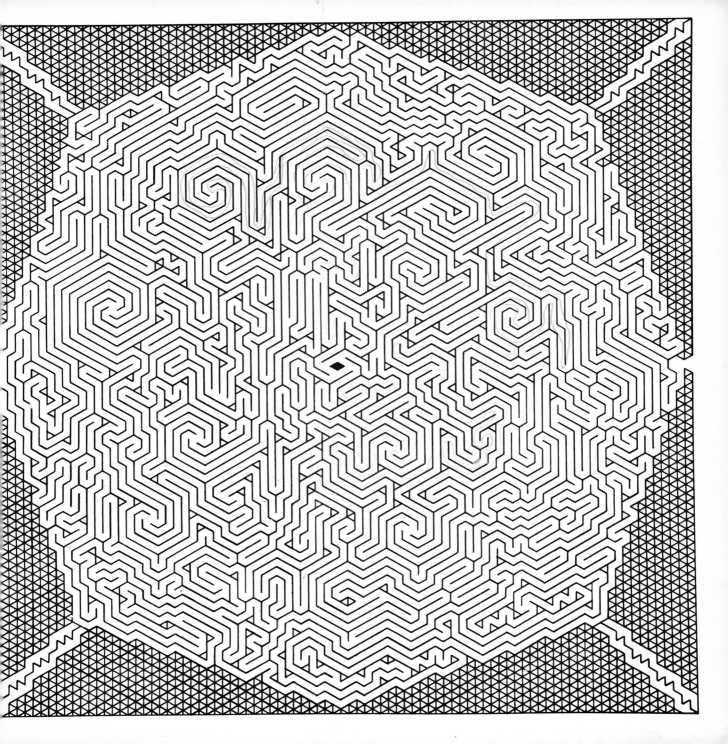

M33 Mutually Accessible Pages

'What good is a book that does not even carry us beyond all books?'*

START IN THE CENTRAL SQUARE OF THE FIRST PAGE.

END IN THE CENTRAL SQUARE OF THE FOURTH PA

* Nietzsche, *The Gay Science,* Bk III, 248

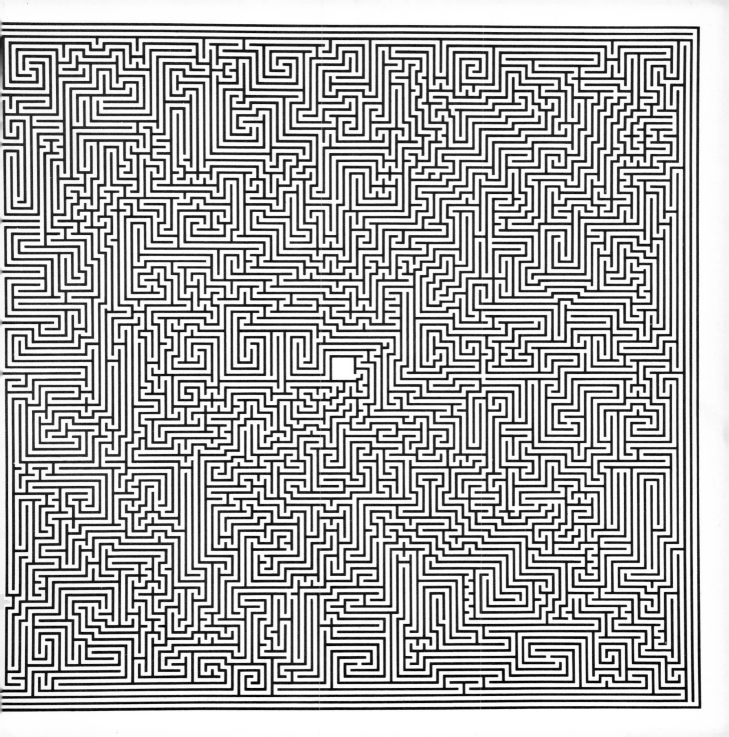

M35 The Second Enantiomorph Maze

You can't hear everything you believe. These ears have walls.

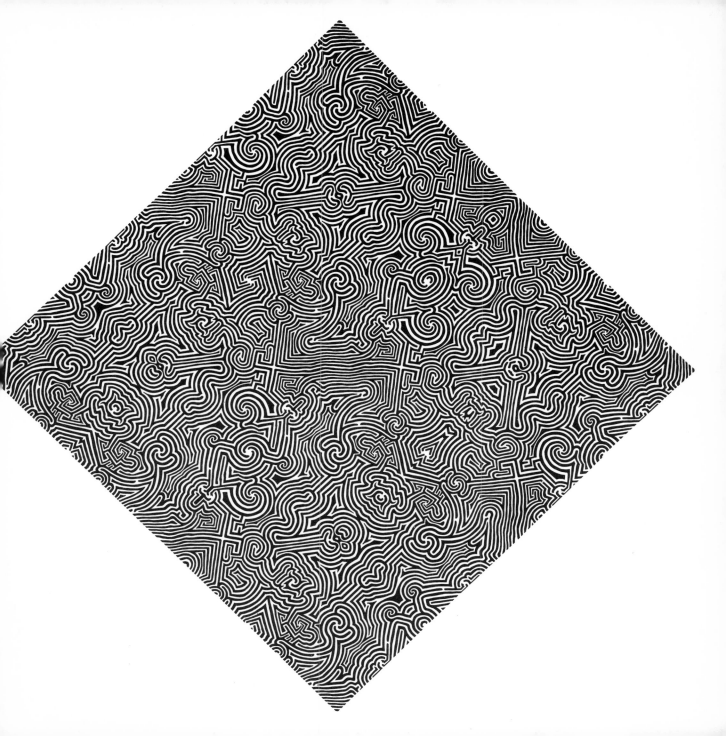

M1

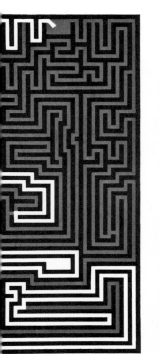

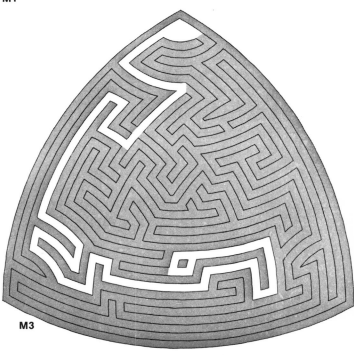

M3

M4

M5

M6

M7

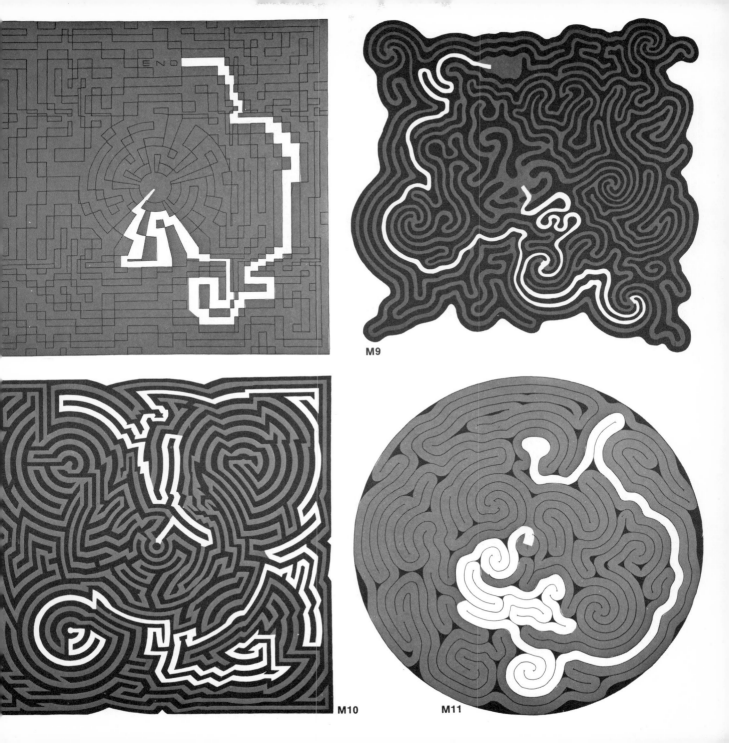

M9

M10

M11

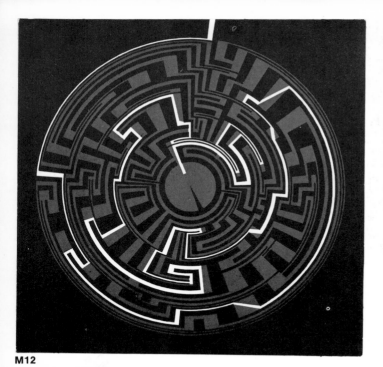

M12

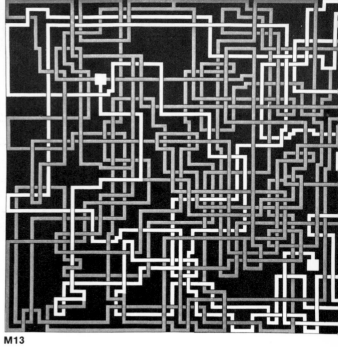

M13

M14

M15

M17

M18

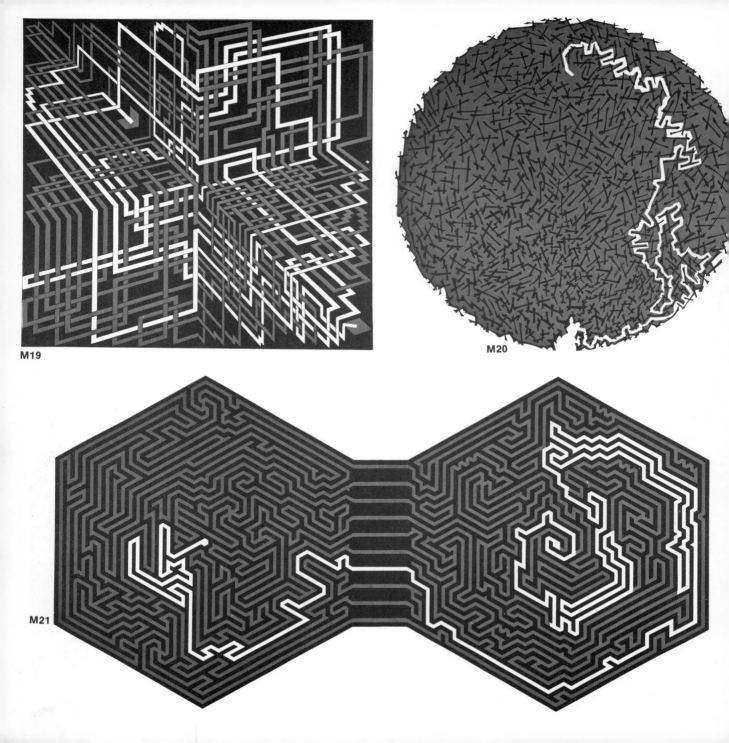

M19

M20

M21

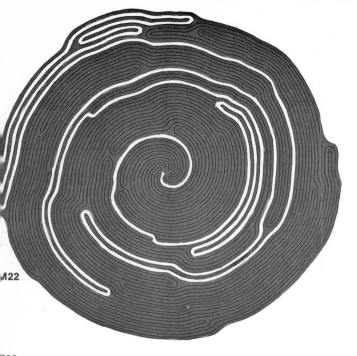

M22

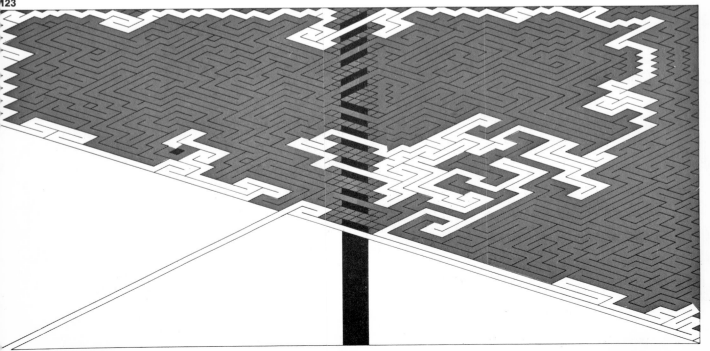

M23

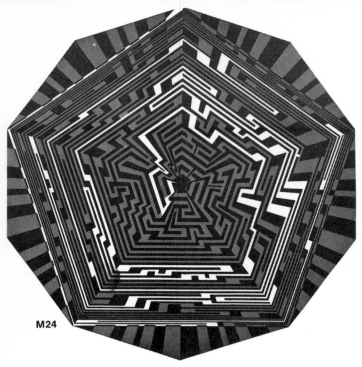

M24

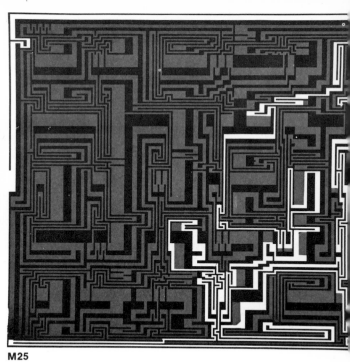

M25

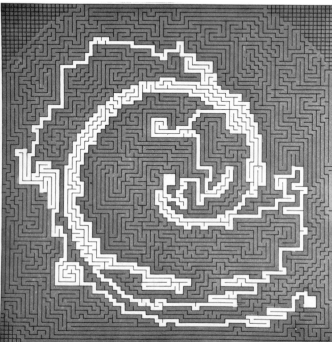

M26

M27